Corazon and the Mestiza

Corazon and the Mestiza

Joel Gaines

RESOURCE *Publications* • Eugene, Oregon

CORAZON AND THE MESTIZA

Copyright © 2021 Joel Gaines. All rights reserved. Except for brief quotations in critical publications or reviews, no part of this book may be reproduced in any manner without prior written permission from the publisher. Write: Permissions, Wipf and Stock Publishers, 199 W. 8th Ave., Suite 3, Eugene, OR 97401.

Resource Publications
An Imprint of Wipf and Stock Publishers
199 W. 8th Ave., Suite 3
Eugene, OR 97401

www.wipfandstock.com

PAPERBACK ISBN: 978-1-6667-3031-9
HARDCOVER ISBN: 978-1-6667-2162-1
EBOOK ISBN: 978-1-6667-2166-9

SEPTEMBER 14, 2021

Contents

Warmth | 1
Winters Gift | 2
Time Stops | 3
Seeing Red | 4
Independence Day | 5
Outstretched | 6
Stoic Tango | 7
Sacuanjoche | 8
Sandinista | 9
Future Foundation | 10
The Question | 12
Past, Present, or Future? | 14
New Dress | 15
Oppression Will Die | 16
Color Blind | 17
In Between | 18
Insomnia and Saints | 19
Border House | 20
Second Generation | 22
Grateful Tourist | 23

Saint Hand | 24

Blind | 25

Voice | 26

1978 | 27

Two Anthems | 28

Step in Time | 29

Destination Unknown | 30

The Condition | 31

Running Together | 33

The Tree We Sat On | 35

Tell Me | 37

Ashes | 38

Lighting Rod | 39

Grace and Caution | 40

Manakin | 41

Conquistadores | 42

New Wind | 44

Light Pollution | 45

Not Complicated | 46

Warmth

My presence is valley
I am the Río San Juan
The beating heart of the seasons
Motives are never built on cities
They were already here
Mestiza, I am calling
My warmth is inviting
Does the watchmaker set the time?
Or is time meaningless to me?
I move at my pace
My warmth is inviting
Beaming on you
I will expose you
Movement in the shadows
Mestiza, I am calling you
My warmth is inviting
Exposure is never cold
Truth and light hand in hand
Like an ever growing romance
Mestiza, I am calling you
My warmth is inviting
I do not rise
I have always been
Chase me
Mestiza, I am calling you
My warmth is inviting
Let me show you what you can't see
Oh the vanity of the elements
Do not give power to the powerless
Mestiza, call me "Corazon"
My warmth is inviting

Winters Gift

A discovery when I wasn't looking
Those are the rarest kind
Far from home
Across the border
Brought not born
A city covered in snow
Drifts piled high covered in black
Cold winds of winter and parked cars
Dirty boots and worn out jeans
A forecast unpleasant as the suburban glares
Sacred Caribbean breeze
Yes, I can feel it in February
Mestiza, "Did you know that would be the day?"
Corazon, "Did you know that I can dance?"

The journey of the Mestiza
What did you carry on that day?
How heavy was your load?
Did you know, Mestiza, that you would be discovered?

The illumination of the Corazon
What did you carry on that day?
What scars did you hide?
Did you know, Corazon, that you would be discovered?

He is as restless as the nocturnal coyote
She is as obligated as the sun to the platano
Mestiza, "The snow has melted"
Corazon, "My sweet, I will teach you to dance in the sun"

Time Stops

The sun rose in a glorious haze on the time spent.
Thoughts swirling as impulsive as the wind.
Small talk has no home on this bed.
Brown eyes tell the story of a vibrant soul.
Love takes flight.
Passengers from far away stories become and became.
As the horizon continues to fade away, eyes open.
Hands no longer tied.
Two lovers take flight.
Grounded on a simple word said as easy as breathe.
Ever changing horizons cannot condemn the word.
One word to find meaning for miles, memories, moments that stop time
Love has defined us.
Love has moved us.
Love has traveled with us.
Love will usher us.
Where fear and insecurity meets
Love will intrude, interrupt, intercept.

My love, her love,
our love will be.

Seeing Red

With confidence as rare as the warm rain of winter
A Mestiza wearing red
only when it rains
The color of passion
A tone behind the words
words she has never said
"Corazon, I don't know how but I have hidden this"
Some lands are in conflict
Beliefs so strong that emotions are buried
Buried but not deep
Conviction in a time to fight
Seen as a weakness in war
A distraction to what they were fighting for
"Corazon, la vergüenza is at my core."
"Mestiza, I see no value in it."
She always wears red, even when she doesn't
Nicaragua, when you look back, do recognize who you were?
Do you call yourself a victim in war?
When the earth shook, when the storm came, when the bullets
   hit like rain . . . .
"Mestiza, do old wounds sting in the rain?"
She is dressed in red
"Corazon, I know I did the best I can"
Nicaragua, you still stand
"Mestiza, in the night she holds your hand"
Nicaragua, look back to remember
Tell your tales to the young
Let emotions rise and set like the western sun
"Mestiza, your war is over"
Wear red in the rain, wear red in the sun
"Mestiza, peace may have begun"

Independence Day

With open arms
"Corazon, I am home"
With eyes full of questions, while the wind blew on a structure
  where she lays her head
Head winds, with a head full of dreams
A heart with a destination unknown
"Corazon, I must stay for now"
"Mestiza, día de la Independencia is not here yet"
39 years she celebrates
Not looking back
Truth echoes in her words
Nicaragua, you are not a border, not a cause
You are what you have birthed
Labor pains, painstakingly seen in the faces
Young and old
Truth comes from her land
Truth is in the quiet tone
The brown eyes of a dream
"Mestiza, truth is only truth if it is timeless"
"Corazon, together we stop time"
She can cross any border
He can see past the city limits
As she calculates her next move
He can see a blurred vision on next year
"Mestiza, it is not yet día de la Independencia"
He can see it coming as he celebrates the day she was born
Sooner than yesterday
They will rest in each other and say
"Feliz día de la independencia"

Outstretched

Planting roots in a land where her roots can only stretch so far
A vibrant soul confined into four walls she did not build
A transplant on chemically altered soil
As vast as the Mombacho
I walk in her clouds
As gentle as the Heliconia
I smell the courage
She is proud
She is plotting to move
She is pronouncing her intentions
Unstoppable as the San Ramon
I will listen to her waters
I will admire her strength
If I am shined upon
I will be an intention

Stoic Tango

Telling stories sad enough to be true
Steps of perseverance higher than the Mogoton
She is still breathing
The "experts don't know how"
A stoic grace of the Tango she once loved
He listens in awe
Gently reaching for her hand
Like a doe of Rapidan at the streams
He speaks to affirm the saddest of songs
He attempts to expose courage
The hesitating beauty touching his lips
They sun may never set over the Las Pilas
She says with authority like he's never heard it
"Corazon, you are not thinking"
But his heart is beating like the day he was born

Sacuanjoche

"Corazon, the distance is hard, My Love."
"Mestiza, please never let the season determine hope"
If painful winds bring thought to you
Let them pass
If eyes of a further horizon tempt you
Don't ignore the beauty in front of you
Like a slow drip of morning dew
Believe that Sacuanjoche can bloom in winter.
And if they do, hold on
The roots may be the strongest

Sandinista

There are no fortunes in war
Just like in a civil war, no civil rights
Shout "Sandinista."
Little ears can't truly pick sides
But they can cover them

It's 2am. She says "Corazon, it happened again"
Cold sweats and realistic visions
As her heart beats, the shaking stalls
The scars of children sometimes never heal

He sleeps through her pain
He rises and his heart sinks
"Darlin, I got scars too, from a different war."
He wishes her peace but deep down
He knows it won't fully heal the scars

She bleeds for him
He aches for her
With the optimism of young soldiers
They believe love can be the true revolution.

Future Foundation

Have you ever been told to smile, Mestiza?
Without an inquiry of your condition?
Requesting a manufactured emotion is an insult to the organic
Roots can run deep
They can be the deepest when planted by waters
Fertile soil
Allowing a foundation to grow
Digging deeper in stubborn pride to not be shaken
Have you ever been told to breathe?
Without an inquiry of your condition?
The measure of roots is found in the wind
Gut winds
From every direction they come
Dancing to their own song
The cold winds cut
The warm winds comfort
"Corazon, how are my roots now?"
As the winds come and go
Ask questions
Feel
The tragic nature of gut winds
Sometimes they come for the young
Gut winds in the young will return
Gut winds will attempt to sabotage
Gut winds will attempt to perplex
Gut winds will attempt to overtake
The premeditated assault of the gut wind
Waiting for the perfect time
When you feel planted
When you feel roots growing strong
When you feel connected

When you are planted in new soil
Take your time by the waters
Dig in deeper
Allow yourself to stand
Test what you see
Hold on to what is given
If you know it is good
"Mestiza, I will wait
For as long as it takes
If you are willing
And plant roots with you"

The Question

I see you looking back at me
I hear the volume of your stare
I feel your intentions
I smell your independence
I taste the air you consume
I touch the last moment we were here
I think I know you

We were talkers and liars
We were authors of our own narrative
We were hopeless romantics
We were soldiers in a war we created
We fought blow by blow
We were young and did not know it
We were daydreamers by day and dancers by night

Our Road was wide
Our path was clear
Our coordinates embedded in us
Our positioning chased the sun
Our guide was the wind
Our map was our heart
Our compass was true north

Self sufficient
Self indulgent
Self defense
Self esteem
Self serving
Self reliable
Self sustaining

Time to tighten my laces
Time to look ahead
Time to show you
Time to teach you
Time to lead all
Time to be in front
Time to be admired

One question before I go
"Mestiza, can you help me breathe?"

Past, Present, or Future?

To think about you
To look ahead
It might be too much, darlin

"Corazon, what about my gut?
It might be all I have and all I know"

Stand on the tracks
Watch the train go by
Old smoke and future destinations

Darlin, I could go back
Down every splintered track
Turn over every stone under broken bottles

I could jump on that train
Tell you what I see
But that would leave you without me
"Corazon, I am glad you are in it now"

In this moment
Let the past breeze by
Let the fuel burn at is own pace
She will not jump
He will not run
At the crossing
In this moment
They will see each other

New Dress

She has a new dress
softest Mestiza skin
with brown curls flowing like the Cascada de San Ramon
a steady stream flowing south, from the heart of where she was
   born
"Corazon, I have not danced in years!"
Tonight, Mestiza, you did dance
You dance as you breathe
Acclimation is an insult
"Mestiza, acclimation is survival for you"
in my land we want her to dance
as long as we pick the song
I spend time in the sun
in a field that I work with guilty hands
Do you know where she came from?
The land of perseverancia
We ask her to acclimate
with our customs, we ask her to suffocate
"Corazon, my legs are tired"
"Mestiza, teach me to dance"

Oppression Will Die

"Corazon, I have to trust my instincts"
instinctively he questions
"Mestiza, are your instincts a means to an end?"
His head sinks to stare at the concrete
Surrounded by high rises and ambitions
of those who have trampled on her people
She thinks of the dirt roads of home
with Nicaraguan dust still on her feet
"Corazon, my intentions are pure. Never do I want to hurt you!"
They have gathered by the thousands
in the streets of dust
Ortega, you also have intentions
to silence the opposition
only to take what land they have built
"Corazon, I have been wounded"
"Mestiza, never has that stopped your intentions"
As they gathered in dissent
the cowards troops gathered weapons
yet they still gathered
streets fill with the blood of the brave
Dead and wounded
"Mestiza, I see your pain, as you hear them cry"
with instinct they fight
Nicaragua, oppression will die

Color Blind

In a crowd she sees colors
He sees hers is the brightest one
A proud Mestiza in a land I am not proud of
"Corazon, my people are different, tolerant"
"Mestiza, I cannot say the same"
Nicaragua, are you as blue as your flag?
A nation built on colors
Through the hardships of war
In the midst of oppression
Does your heart still beat for equality?
He holds her close
She holds onto every word
"Corazon, I must be guarded. I have to"
He sees color in a different light
The blind light of those who stare
"Mestiza, I know you are not from here. I would curse the day, if
 you never came!"
"Corazon, today I am aware of the color of my skin"
My people have made her aware
What is the color of shame?
What color defines the thoughts behind blind eyes?
With shame he only wants to see the color of her eyes
"Mestiza, eres una inspiración!"
Nicaragua, does tolerance still define you?
In my land, I fear we are blind

In Between

I heard your words today
now I can clearly see
"Mestiza, you are stuck in between"
a Madroño planted in a climate
planting shallow roots
"Corazon, I need to check the temperature"
growing taller to feel the breeze
roots stretching into the unwelcoming soil
Madrono, you have stretched your roots until the end
this land has not been kind
Gracefully you have worked this land
with all that have walked past you
with vile stares
the blind swing of an angry ax
racist attempt to cut you down
"Mestiza, they cannot cut what is inside"
"Corazon, I have acclimated to your land. My roots will never die"
"Mestiza, you have carried the weight of in between"
Growing taller in a country
Rooted in home
"These are my people, Corazon"
"Mestiza, I know home is calling and home you see"
Madrano, for as long as you stand in my land
"Corazon, rest your tired bones on me"

Insomnia and Saints

as night fell some did sleep
a familiar slumber in the comfort of the Nicaraguan heat
as night fell for the bravest ones
a new day begins
they held the rosary with eyes full of tears
looking for a country they have never met
they felt the tears of the Saints hit the floor
a time for mourning in the night
lasting for a moment
an exit, a passage to a right
"Corazon, I will not stay much longer"
"Mestiza, how you have grown
Nicaragua, you have a country, for some not a home
he said with a voice from the lowlands
"Corazon, I have loved before, this time I feel something more"
As some sleep while awake
the most courageous dream
they see beyond what is present
a sanctifying theme
"Mestiza, I see how you have grown, beyond the suburban
   settlement you have known"
"Corazon, this is our time, this love is awake"
this love is our home

Border House

Borders are funny
as silly as politics
As useless as those who hide behind them
cowards who "cry freedom!"
but not louder than the children who cry
Uncle Sam builds a house
with his long patriotic arms
he rips the children from those who seek you
Borders are funny, in the saddest way
We all are simple beings walking a planet
Humans who are funny, spending an eternity
defining rights
Tell me who gave you permission?
who gave you life?
One last question?
who gave you the right?
Words can be funny
The comedians who ignore the cries
name children "unaccompanied"
Qait, one more question
how did they earn that name?
a vile attempt to cause harm, and ask a victim to apologize
Tell me a story Uncle Sam,
tell me why a human would leave a homeland?
tell me why a mother would run to you?
tell me the part why a father would lose his life to seek you?
and tell me, Uncle Sam,
how did you greet them when they met you?
I want to know your greatest achievement
how do you ignore the cries of children?
Is it because you never listened why they ran to you?

Dear Uncle Sam,
Please "document" this.
When did your heart unaccompany you?

Second Generation

Please help me untie this knot
my stomach twisting as I hear the news
the actions of children, a reaction to an environment
"Corazon, she never asked for any of this"
Managua, what stories do you tell your young?
unfiltered songs they have sung
to then be told what to sing
we fought bravely for freedom to ring
"Corazon, I had different path, an easy road"
"Mestiza, how she has your heart"
Managua, from your ashes you have risen
But do your children know what you have built?
or do they dwell in the works of your hands
what was never given, is now a hand out
"Corazon, she must be strong, she has too!"
Ortega, with every lie you fix the fight
hoping those who give life will ignore human rights
"Corazon, I cannot always rescue her"
"Mestiza, you have shown her"
Nicaragua, do not ignore your young
Managua, never forget the endless fight
against the weapons, the acts of nature, and the complacency that
   turns bright eyes into night
Teach your young about your fight, passed down to you
Nicaragua, never give in
Children gather to claim your birthright!

Grateful Tourist

Mestiza is feeling again
Never to guard her heart
Is it a job or a mission?
A question that needs no answer
She feels
She gives like the waters of the Coco river
The heart of the Mestiza will carry on
Head strong as the Western Mountains
Hands as deep as the Caribbean

I am a tourist
In awe of the illumination
If l stand in the valley of Jalapa
I profit from the workers hands
I am a tourist
In love with her hands

Saint Hand

Santiago, how big are your palms?
Do you hold Managua in your hand?
Shall I celebrate the Mestiza or honor what is is your hand?
If I grip too tight she may fade away
If I open my palm she may reach for me
If I fall she may catch me with her hand
Tonight on this tree I want to never let go
Mestiza, what do you hold close?
Santiago, what have you seen?
Do you smile at the courage of the Mestiza?
Or do you hesitate because you know what is to come?
She says "I am happy to see you"
He says "I do not ever want to look away"
Mestiza, place your hand in mine
I will not grip too tight
Santiago, please never let her go

Blind

to reconcile is to give birth
labor pains, the work is painful
"I am moving from shame to healing, Corazon"
she speaks freely with no government
remember the people of the Nicaraguan sun
saw no government, only corruption
capitalists only capitalize on what they think they can conquer
"It has taken me seven years, Corazon"
she speaks with a tone like the day they won
what she has revolutionized can't be bought
the movement can fade as quickly as it came
as subtitle as the day she walked away
"Mestiza, it may not be the best of times"
and He rules the land, forgetting that corruption is what makes a
   people blind
speak loud while silencing your own kind
Mestiza, I am blind
let not my words stop what has begun
"Corazon, this is healing"
day one

Voice

Voracious is her voice
in my land we define "freedom"
teach our young to sing to you
freedom is the right to never be silent
oh how life has tried!
"Corazon, I have had these thoughts"
she calls them trauma
a watered-down reference from my land
to define the scars in one word
is to speak without substance
Nicaragua, He is trying to silence you!
from his mansion he declares his intentions
from the hills to the ocean waters
wounds are weapons
He screams at the San Cristobal
"Stay silent!"
ignoring the heart of a nation
erupting at any moment
"Soon, Mestiza, comes your moment"
in my land they want to silence her
yet call her free
"Mestiza, you will not be defeated"
Nicaragua, you will not be silenced
"Mestiza, your freedom I see"

1978

The year of revolution
1978 when an idea became fate
The struggle of millions
a fire inside
when you look back on fate
on the birth date,
do you see the work had just begun?
love wins always because it won
"Mestiza, tell me what you reorganize"
Sleepless night and what you cannot hide
"Oh Corazon, sometimes I do the math"
Loving the revolution
Waiting for the future
Fearing the Aftermath
"Corazon, does it hurt you?"
"Mestiza, I won't die without you"
Moving to the shade, sometimes afraid of the sun
"I don't want to live without you"
you can take two steps back
"Mestiza, I won't run"

Two Anthems

She said "will you walk with me?
I want to tell you stories of the old country"
"My roots run deep, Corazon"
Two anthems, one older and one sweeter

She said "I used to sing the old one"
He thought "she has a lot to sing about now"
She said "my face didn't fall down"
He said "I can't stop looking."

She said "the struggle has been corrupted"
With one look she told a story of a thousand soldiers
She said "Corazon, I want to take you there"

She said "I feel powerless"
He said "it's hard, darlin, with no end in sight."
He looked In her eyes and felt the struggle of a thousand
    thoughts.

She said "I am wearing red today."
He picked up his head
She said "I can picture us both in that valley"
He said "I will go anywhere with you, darlin"

He said "darlin, I am here."
She said "for four nights I dreamed of you."
He said "we got this. "
They said "I love you."

Step in Time

She taught me to dance before she caught a train
"Corazon, stay off the tracks"
"Mestiza, I hope you dance on the roof tonight"
Count the steps, keep step in time
Eight counts, two counts, the way she moves
It is what counts
"When you see me again I will be older"
Her mind dances with revolution
Thoughts of what she has been
Keep step in time
"Mestiza, it is your time"
She recalls a different time
She plots how to get back to her
The train has left that time
A long track
She gets off the train
Declares this "my stop"
"Corazon, now I will walk"
Walking her own path
No conductor
No instructor
"This dance I will lead"
One step, into two
I will watch her dance
See her move
Sitting back with a smile
"Corazon, take my hand, move me, and I will move you"

Destination Unknown

"The roads to most places in my land are unpaved and dangerous, Corazon."
Is the distance worth it?
Two travelers with bags packed
Destination unknown
Known obligations packed full
"I sleep on your side of the bed, Corazon, to smell you"
How one sense of smell can inhale the peace of home
"Mestiza, I did sleep on your side"
True love is not pressure
Only the desire of a traveler
"Mestiza will we get to see the rainforest? Or will we fall from the cliffs?"
The wise may tell us to guard our hearts
For they have been spectators watching travelers fall
Maybe they have never loved at all
The free need no guard rails
Until I can travel to you
I will circle the land
Alone
While thoughts of you orbit
Dreaming that we will land

The Condition

Rights of spring give birth to you
Born in April, as most great movements
Waking up to corruption, calling out for something more
Nicaragua heard you cry
From the hills of the illiterate
the broken read the moment
Nobody is born alone
"Corazon, I want to go home"
From the hills they stayed silent
From their homes they left in the night
Passion orbits movement
With nothing left to lose
April gives birth to the greatest of fighters
With the first step of courage,
More courage seen in any man
"Mestiza, home is not a location, but a condition"
Oh how they fought
Outnumbered, outside the lines
The Mestiza of April does not look for war
In her blood she has the fight
the two faces of a memory
one face of truth
Corazon faces her
She touches his face
The gentlest of battle scared hands
Hands of a lover and fighter
Corazon's face after the battle
Simple smile of a touch
Facing each other
Rise together

The Sandinista is here
"Corazon, tell me what you know!"
"Mestiza, you are home"

Running Together

Migrate to me, Mestiza
Open your arms, Corazon
Reach for me with an outstretched soul
Peak over the horizon
The best scene is around the corner
You cannot see it
Your ancestors have hoped for it
Have told stories of landing and rooting
Uproot your tired feet Mestiza
I will land
In your land
In my land
We can land
She says "Corazon, I keep them at arm's length"
"Mestiza, I am in your arms"
Have you seen the clouds build over Honduras?
Have you seen the slow moving rain from the East? The clouds slowly crawl over the Caribbean waters?
Gathering strength with the palate of organic pigmentations
Do you move towards the cooling breeze?
Or do we stand in wait?
We shall let the sun warm us
If we stay too long we will stop chasing the other side.
"Corazon, let me tell you about the frown! Oh how I wanted to run from you."
"Mestiza, but where would you run?"
We could circle the landscape and never have the courage to cross the border.
Mestiza, take a step forward
Take two steps back
I will stand next to you

I will wait in the clouds
I will get burned in the summer sun
We will walk together
In any season
In any climate
Our love will be free
Free to stay

The Tree We Sat On

When you put your feet on my land, what did you feel, Mestiza?
Did you cross a border? Into a new land?
You are not a stranger
A fierce lover
A proud fighter
A self protector
With a new reach
Did you see how the Blue Heron's nest?
Did you see how they protect the young?
Does it remind you of your ancestors?
The ones who were home
The proud citizens who rose to become soldiers?
We hid together on my land
Although we were not hiding
Did you feel the weight lifted as we shared?
The tree we sat on fell for us.
For years it waited
The tree refused to die
Until it gave us life
We made our bed
Covered ourselves in stories
Blanketed in passion
Mestiza, do you know a naked smile stops thought?
Managua, are your arms as open as her heart?
She says "I don't want to hurt you, Corazon. I will not."
"Mestiza, I believe you"
The Mestiza told me of old wounds
with a voice of certainty
With the grace of the doe that passed us
We could be predators hungry for a kill
The doe never lost sight of the slow moving stream

You have not lost your voice
In this field, Mestiza, we found a collective voice
A together voice
"Corazon, I will not let that happen"
"Mestiza, I believe you"
I will not retrace this path
Nicaragua, footsteps do not fade in the summer sun
Nor does the love of the Mestiza
"Mestiza, you were here"
"Corazon, I am"

Tell Me

Tell me, Mestiza, what drives you?
Is it the land that gave you life or the life you give this land?
Tell me, Mestiza, what have you overcome?
Is it the pain you see or the pain you feel?
Tell me, Mestiza, where do you find your heart?
Is home where the heart is or has this land been heartless?
Tell me, Mestiza, how do you love?
Your head, heart, hands, or all of the above?
Tell me, Mestiza, who will you be?
The pain of the past or the victory I see
Tell me, Mestiza, do you know who I am?
The Corazon who celebrates you in his land!

Ashes

May I have a word?
No please, I need one
I heard the news
I her it in her tone
The San Cristobal is raining ash again
Mestiza "how are you feeling tonight?"
Did you feel the lava spill over?
Are you standing in the ash?
Mestiza, do you know something is burning?
The lava is boiling
Crawling down the mountain you once climbed
Mestiza "do you feel it?"
I want a language of my own
I want burning words that feel like winds of change
I want a tongue only you understand
Mestiza said "we all have those moments Corazon."
Something is burning in your eyes.
"Corazon, I like the rain"
Surrounded by the ashes she says
"I see you."

Lighting Rod

Oh great land look what you have birthed?
Nicaragua, your borders can not contain her
Burst with lighting on that day
Someone caught that bolt
Brought her to America
A fire never to be covered.
Try and cut her hair. Slow her feet.
She rises again. And again.
Tell her what you see. Give her your narrow insight. Try and mold her to this land.
Fool yourself and yell at the lighting to stop
Stand in the tropical winds and scream louder
Elect a racist to represent you
He will build a wall to contain the sky and then cry when he is defeated.
I will laugh with her
Your fallacy is not her reality
The Nicaraguan lighting struck me in my land
Damn I tried to lie to the weather
I laugh at my efforts
Mestiza eyes looking at me
A voice bathed in stories of pain and glory
My ears are opened
I live in a field
I am a lighting rod
She calls me Corazon

Grace and Caution

Standing tall, with curls of courage
The color of her face is not to be duplicated
She is a woman with footprints on several shores
She says what is overwhelming
She says "I need to slow down"
A fierce heart always has scars
As those who have lived always have stories
He stands tall
Loving the sun on his skin
He is a man with memorials
Like ebenezer stones planted
What do you tell your children?
The Corazon is a hopeless romantic
The Mestiza can always dance
Corazon moves with restless feet
Mestiza moves with grace and caution
Corazon resists the shade in the heat of the day
Mestiza dances with control hidden to the naked eye
Corazon finds the medlar el árbol
Mestiza says "Corazon, I will teach you to dance"
Corazon says "if only you will dance with me"
From afar or in each other's arms
They both ask to keep step in time
In those moments
they will not "pass the time"
Time will stop

Manakin

Rise, Manakin, and take flight
With colors as glorious as the fight
When did you first fly?
What caught your eye?
Was it the Indio Maiz?
Did your first flight pause?
Was the first sight rare?
Did you feel the Caribbean air?
Manakin, did you dance in the migration?
Manakin, have you reached your destination?
Manakin, did you fall in love without hesitation?
Oh brown eyes you said "Corazon, I don't think I have been in
  love before. I don't want to say anymore."
He reflects at a later time
"I have but who is keeping score?"
Can the Manakin compare the Indio Maiz and the first sight of
  the Río San Juan?
At the sound of her voice, the touch of her hand, smell of her hair,
  love in her words
He thinks "This is my first flight"
Vulnerability
The freedom of ability
Overthinking complexity
The Manakin soars
Quiet the mind, stop the fight
Corazon and the Mestiza say
"I just want to lay next to you tonight."

Conquistadores

Have you seen the way the sun shines through the shade?
Have you seen how the sun shines on your organic smile in the morning?
With an instant, her smile fades
Returning maybe even quicker

The conquistadores invade with strength
They invade with purpose
They invade with lies to not they believe

With her, they have no heart
With strength rarely seen
She will not fight
She will not complain
She will not call for help
She knows the only weapon to destroy the heartless
She knows the weapon will strike several small blows
Slowly bleeding the conquistadors
She will not go for the heart
They have none

He will lay next to her
He speak of past victims of the conquistadors
He will share his weapons
They may not be as sharp
But he knows that hers are shaper
He knows that with small strokes of courage
The cowards will run
The cowards will sail away

He will tell the story of her heart
He will ask her if he can be a witness
He will ask her if he can be the scribe
He will ask for her heart
And on that morning
The sun will shine on them both

New Wind

The early spring ocean breezes through her brown hair
She sits and thinks about the winds of old
But feels new
Gone are the loved ones
The memories will dwell in her
Like the Zapatera Archipelago waters
The ripples of white that have left her a path
Ancient ruins aren't ruined at all
He sits in the sun
He hears the news she is at peace
The old winter winds are subtly fading
Ancient ruins and volcanic ash build monuments that grieve and celebrate the old
They both look at the same sun
Believing they can build something new

Light Pollution

She can't see the stars in the city
The orange light shines on parked cars in a stalled traffic jam
Brown eyes turning red
Obligations mocking her dreams
On her porch, the concrete is never translucent
Steady in blocking the horizon
She wakes from her dream
Feeling powerless as she cannot yet see the horizon
He can see the stars
Light pollution miles away
Naked feet settled in the grass
Virgin wind tunnels through a beard of grey
He thinks of her
He thinks of today
Translucent honestly
The only kind
He cannot see the horizon
Yet
Believing that she might see it first
With certainty, an out stretched hand
Fully convinced
Together they will see red eyes fall away
Together they will be

Not Complicated

Defeat is not complicated
"Corazon, I had a new feeling today"
His heart skips a beat, unknown if fear or joy would greet him
"I felt small today"
His heart began to sink
As he pondered the reason for a tragic thought
"I let it pass, Corazon"
"Mestiza, I want to know."
"It has passed my love"
With a voice as strong as the country she came from
"I will not be defeated"
Simple power burning like the Mayan sun
Contained in summer skin
just like the first time he heard her say "Corazon"
"Mestiza, I have no doubt"
Those who doubt, fear defeat
The one who rules the land
scared of those just like her
constructing new laws
manipulating words into policy
holding onto power
the grip of a coward
afraid of the defeat that waits
Defeat is not complicated
You will be defeated
Nicaragua, you never will
"Mestiza, your courage is simple"
Like the beating heart of a nation
"Corazon, look how far you have come!"
"Mestiza, may your courage take us farther"

www.ingramcontent.com/pod-product-compliance
Lightning Source LLC
Chambersburg PA
CBHW071405160426
42813CB00084B/529